MW01169306

ISBN: 9781313467797

Published by:
HardPress Publishing
8345 NW 66TH ST #2561
MIAMI FL 33166-2626

Email: info@hardpress.net
Web: http://www.hardpress.net

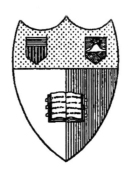

The Philosophy of Business

A LITTLE BOOK FOR BIG MEN

by

A. B. FRANCISCO

ag. 1 0 3 3 1

WM. H. POOL PRINTING & BINDING CO.
626 S. CLARK ST,   CHICAGO, U. S. A.

TO MY SON

MERCER,

AND ALL BUSINESS MEN WHO DESIRE TO
WIN LIFE'S BATTLES THROUGH THE DE-
VELOPMENT OF THEIR VIRTUES, AND
WHO ALSO BELIEVE THAT NATURE'S
LAWS ARE DIVINE.

CONTENTS

PREFACE

THE business world is fast awakening to the fact that business is a science. Indeed, many minds have presented business as a science in such able and praiseworthy ways that the idea is now becoming universally accepted. But as far as the author knows, the *philosophy* underlying this new and dynamic science has not been written. In the interest of individual and co-operative success, he has attempted, in this little book for big men, to give the true philosophy of business. He considers business in the sense of a world-wide form of *busy-ness,* involving service as the fundamental principle.

He sees in business a melting-pot, or crucible, into which men and women are forced by the laws of nature and submitted to the acid test of merit, *the survival of the serviceable.* Success results from the development of the virtues in obedience to natural laws as written in the constitutions of both nature and human nature. He relies upon the innate selfishness of the individual to counteract and restrain organized greed, that fair play may eventually be given to all. Finally, a perfect society will be evolved which will reflect the sovereignty of God in an industrial democracy. Thus business is seen to be the dynamic science which will regenerate the race.

THE AUTHOR.

Chicago, May 13, 1916.

CHAPTER I.

THE BUSINESS WORLD'S AWAKENING

The times do change and we should change with them.
—Shakespeare.

"TO UNDERSTAND our relation to the history of humanity and to test our hopes for the future," let us imagine with Professor Heinrich Schmidt, a pupil of Haeckel, "a gigantic clock that records, not minutes but centuries, and that the whole history of mankind is crowded into twenty-four hours. Let us assume that we are living in the noon hour of this long human day, and accordingly measure the progress of the human race."

Professor James Harvey Robinson, of Columbia University, has made the reckoning suggested, and states that "Man has been standing upright and seeking out inventions for approximately two hundred forty thousand years. Each hour on the history clock, thus represents twenty thousand years, each minute three centuries, and each second five years. In this long human day nothing is recorded up to half past eleven. At twenty minutes to twelve the earliest Babylonian and Greek culture began to appear; Greek philosophy was born ten minutes before twelve. It is only three minutes since we began to make the steam engine do our work. It was only two minutes before twelve when the idea of conscious progress entered the mind of man. We have been awake, figuratively speaking, scarcely more than a minute."

This is a graphic and forceful illustration of how slowly the race-mind unfolds itself; but now that it is awakened, it progresses with such incredible rapidity that the twentieth century shines with greater light than all the two thousand four hundred centuries preceding. Witness the marvelous and rapid advance in the sciences of geology, botany, chemistry, mathematics, physics, *et cetera*. The development of each science is like the discovery of a new world, and its applied knowledges are like the peopling of that world, and the filling of it with new life and love and joy.

Looking back over the long and devious road that lies between the barbarism of the past and the civilization of the present, thinking of the centuries that roll like ocean waves between these distant shores, we can form some idea of what our fathers suffered and be led to appreciate the blessed privileges we, their children, should enjoy. It is a long way from the savage to the scientist; from the cliff den to the brown stone mansion; from leaves to garments; from the flickering pine knot to the tungsten light; from the stone hammer to the modern factory; from the dugout log to the Lusitania; from the sickle to the self-binder; from hieroglyphics to the library; from the courier to the telegram; from the echo to the phonograph; from the trumpet to the telephone; from the fallen tree to the suspension bridge; from the sling to the Krupp gun; from revenge to law; from the club to the court; from despotism to democracy; from superstition to science; from might to right; from hate to love.

So much for man's intellectual, scientific, political, economical and ethical development, and his progress in business relations has been equally marvelous and in every way as extraordinary. It is a wide difference between the slogan of the fifteenth century, which was, *"Caveat emptor"* (Let the buyer beware), and the slogan of the twentieth century which is, "He profits most who serves best." The awakening may not be observed by the common mind; the business man himself may not clearly discern the evolution which has been going on for many years, transforming and eventually transfiguring the sordid and servile business world into a form of beauty, and filling it with the spirit of joy.

The sun which lights the way of all human progress is science. Not until very recently have its fair rays shone with enough effulgence in the business mind to separate its firmament of greed from the firmament of use. When we reflect how the sciences of astronomy, navigation and engineering have transformed the material world from a chaos of darkness, superstition and dread, into an order of light, knowledge and joy, in the movements of men in their interests over land and sea, then we see in comparison what is possible to the business world when it, too, will be illuminated by the light of science. Indeed, the search-light of analysis has already been focused upon it, and it is responding to revelation after revelation that is being made. Its mighty forces are being reduced to order, and its wonderful activities directed toward human betterment. Its doubts, fears and cruelties are being transformed into certainties, hopes and blessings. In the realm of business, too, natural laws are seen to reign with the fixedness of gravitation, and their mighty powers, directed with the accuracy of the planets' movements, are as beneficent as the healing dew.

Business is defined by Webster as that which occupies the time, attention and labor of one as his chief concern. Science is organized knowledge, and therefore, the science of business is that organized knowledge which directs one in occupying his time, devoting his attention and expending his labor upon the particular thing which is his chief concern.

From creation's dawn men have been in business, or at least they have been busy,—not about business, but rather busy in avoiding giving their time, attention and labor to any concern. Instead of making a study of how to apply their time, attention and labor to some use *per se,* they have spent their energies in avoiding uses; they have sought to obtain the maximum of return from a minimum of expenditure, to get something for nothing. Exploitation and conquest have been the methods, not only of pirates and warriors but of commercial men, statesmen and ministers.

The light of the twentieth century has revealed to us that those who have enjoyed success have obeyed natural laws and reaped the results thereof. They have observed the fundamental truths: the science of business is the science of service; he profits most who serves best; human welfare is the true basis of prosperity; true competition is creative and not destructive; true salesmanship is not conquest but co-operation. Men who recognize these truths and understand that business is a science, no longer sit idly by the road of commerce with outstretched hands and hats, nor seek gifts and bonuses from city, state or national governments.

The scientific business man is in training to serve. He is studious of an opportunity to supply some need of an ever-growing and perfecting society; he is ever watchful to cut down waste and to take up slack, to reduce lost motion and otherwise to gather up the fragments of preceding centuries of incompetency and sloth. He purposes to attain success by the development of his virtues, rather than to profit by his vices.

CHAPTER II.

THE BUSINESS MAN'S SERVICE

Over and over the task was set;
  Over and over I slighted the work;
But ever and always I know that yet
  I must face and finish the thing I shirk.
                    —*Ella Wheeler Wilcox.*

THE great awakening that the business world is experiencing is due to a vital principle working at the root of human thought and activity, unconsciously, possibly, but producing the results, nevertheless, that we witness. This vital principle is service. Mankind in general, and each individual in particular demands that not only things but other persons serve him. Thus, the universal desire to enjoy life that can come only through things and persons serving him leads to the discovery of the law of *the survival of the serviceable* working out its perfect ends.

Nature does not finish her work, as has been observed, "Nature unaided fails." That is, she fails of complete and perfect ends. This is due to the fact of her relation to man, who is her complement and whose perfection is the end she has in view. She means that man shall become a partner with her and share the responsibility, honor, and glory of completed acts. His selection must perfect her selection and his law must perfect her law. The book of man's life is the record of the laws of cause and effect. He is bound by the cords he weaves out of the woof-thoughts and -feelings as they are enmeshed in the warp of circumstances.

Every created thing is its own peculiar form of service. The mineral kingdom serves the vegetable; the vegetable serves the animal and the animal serves man. Thus, everything serves and in turn is served, by every other thing. "See all things for my use!" "See man for mine!" replies a pampered goose: Since it is true that he profits most who serves best, it is important that we consider the nature of service.

We cannot look to our educational institutions for much information on the subject of service in business. The schools teach a great deal about the natural sciences, but little about business. This is because heretofore business has not been looked upon as a science; it has been generally believed that its truths were to be learned only through experience. This belief is being recognized as erroneous, for men have analyzed business and have found that success in it is governed by definite laws, and that men can learn to obey them by other means than experience.

There are three requisites of service that the aspirant for business success must have, the *desire*, the *how*, and the *capacity* to serve. As a wrestler who aspires to victory develops the muscles of his body, one who wishes to win life's battles must develop these elements of service, for they are his holds upon the things with which he is to wrestle.

Why should one develop his desire to serve? For three reasons: First, because it is his duty to society. A man is a social being and is related directly and indirectly with all other men, who are under the same laws and are mutually interdependent. He owes a great deal to those who have gone before him, for he inherits the blessings of the past. He owes a great deal to those who succeed him, for he is expected to contribute his share to mankind's progress and at the same time hold in trust the inheritance he receives that he may bequeath it to his successors. He is indebted to his contemporaries, who supply him with the comforts of life and share their portion with him. A deep sense of gratitude should, therefore, inspire him with an insatiable desire to serve.

Second, one should develop the desire to serve because it is human to do so, and is his duty to himself. Service is the only road to perfect manhood, and by the faithful application of his mind to some form of service, a man is raised up out of the pit of his animal nature to the height of his human nature. Animals serve, it is true, but they do not have the desire; they are compelled to by a power outside and above themselves. A man has the power within him to compel himself to serve. This compulsion is not slavery, but true freedom, for the greatest conquest that man has ever made over his brute nature is the development of his desire to serve.

Beside the compelling motive of duty to society and to himself, there is a third reason for a man's acquiring the desire to serve, and that is found in the relation of reward to service. The appeal is to his cupidity, for service will bring him rewards in the form of money and honor, and will secure for him the comforts of mind and body. Service is the only honorable means to obtain wealth, and with it come honor and esteem.

The desire to serve then, is of first importance, although oftimes the last to be fully appreciated. Second to it is the *how* to serve. One should develop his how to serve faculty for the same reasons that he develops his desire to serve. Further, the desire must clothe itself in knowledge in order that it may be properly directed. The *how* involves the giving direction. The desire remains inert until direction is given to it and then it takes the very form of the knowledge that directs it. Therefore, the understanding of man should be developed in order that his desire to serve may not prove barren.

A certain young lady with a genuine desire to serve has recently graduated from college and is thrust upon the world without the knowledge of how to put her desire into effect. She is asked by each prospective employer, What can you do? and her negative answer has failed to secure for her a satisfactory position. Another woman, a young widow, left with but a moderate income, feels the necessity of increasing it as well as employing her time in some gainful occupation. She, too, is asked, What can you do? and her answer has not yet secured a position for her. Both of these estimable young ladies have the desire to serve faculty developed to a high degree, but they lack the wisdom or the how to attain their ends.

Now one may be very anxious to serve and also possess the knowledge to give direction to the desire, yet be unable to put into successful practice these two faculties because he lacks the third, *capacity* to serve. The capacity to do what one desires and knows is the last and perfect measure of manhood. It is the ultimate manifestation of the will and understanding in actual words and deeds. We are what we do. The capacity for sustained effort, the power to render obedience to the last detail, the ability to make the infinitesimal mark the magic touch that completes a chain of actions, is the last and best evidence of service.

Service in itself, is composed of three elements, which enter into the disposition of all goods whether they be ideas, labor or commodities, and these elements are, quality, quantity and manner. Obviously, the quality of the goods must be on a par with competitors, else the inferiority will ruin the sales. The quantity must be just or people will refuse to buy. In the third element is found the greatest latitude of difference in the service rendered by different individuals. There are so many ways in which service can be rendered that every man has an opportunity or gateway opened to him which will lead him to success. In the manner in which they serve their customers lies the secret of many successes. Thus we see that service is the all important thing in business, in fact, in all of man's relations with his fellows, for it enters into every activity in which men engage.

CHAPTER III.

SALESMANSHIP—THE MEASURE OF SERVICE

Let no thing be done except by the perfect laws governing its kind.
—Anon.

SALESMANSHIP is often thought of in the narrow sense of commercial barter and trade, whereas, in its broad sense, it is concerned in all human relationships, and a knowledge of it is of vital importance to everyone who wishes to succeed in life. All things are forms of uses, but lie inert until touched by the hand of man. When man sees in them their potential uses and commands them to become active in performing those uses, he thereby renders them into forms of service. The service he commands them to perform are at first such service as has its beginning and end in himself; but when he sees that he may become an instrument to carry these uses over to another, he becomes a salesman, for salesmanship is the application of service to another, or in other words, the measure of a man's service.

The power of salesmanship is tremendous. It gives direction and puts into execution the desires and ambitions of every human being. Even love, without it is an idle dream, but coupled with it, it sends the knight errant on his quest. Ambition, without salesmanship, is only a flaccid wish; with it, an Alexander conquers the world, or the diplomat obtains a concession from a miscreant nation. In the business world it is the power that keeps in motion the wheels of commerce.

Salesmanship is the agent that brings about reactions between minds. Its analogy in the physical world is presented in the agent in chemical and physical reactions. It unites opposing or indifferent forces. Water can be cooled to a temperature below 32° F. without freezing, but when jarred or a piece of ice is dipped into it, it immediately crystallizes and becomes ice. A spark of fire applied to a drop of gasoline produces an explosion whose force may drive an engine. A piece of iron submerged in acid soon goes into solution. Likewise, salesmanship is the force that makes one mind react on another to the extent that it changes its course; it bends the one in agreement to the other. Salesmanship transforms the static world into a dynamic one; it is the means of elevating man from a state of savagery to one of civilization, wherein he has the desire, ability and power to make application of the things about him to the practical affairs of life.

There are three elements in this application, the things, the motion, and the time required. By things are meant all minerals, vegetables or animals which nature puts at man's disposal, and whatsoever he has manufactured or produced from them. The elements of motion and time are intimately connected, as we know from the study of physics. Motion and moments are derived from the same root word; indeed, the efficacy of a motion is measured by the time it requires for completion. The work day is as fixed a unit in the movements of service as the solar day in the movements of the planet. "Day" is derived from two Hebrew words meaning to make a noise and to be hot. We can see how the hum of the busy day may be heard and the heat of the busy life be seen aglow in the movements of service.

There are three kinds of things that can be sold, commodities, labor and ideas. It is generally considered that the merchant sells commodities, the wage-earner sells his labor and the minister sells ideas, but it is more broadly true that everyone sells something of each in a limited degree. Mr. Edison has sold all in a marked degree. Few other men have furnished the world with such an abundance of ideas. It is said that he frequently labors eighteen hours a day, and his commodities illuminate the high and low places from the Statue of Liberty to private pantries, drive innumerable conveyances and mighty wheels of industry; and are heard in private drawing-rooms and public halls. He who possesses no ideas has little to offer in the way of labor or commodities, but he who is possessed of ideas may have much of both labor and commodities.

In making a sale of anything, there are four factors involved: the salesman, the goods, the patron, and the sale. The salesman should qualify himself to handle the other three, by knowing his goods and his patron, and how to bring about an agreement of the patron's mind with his own on the goods, which is the sale.

The sale is brought about in four steps, and the salesman leads the patron in taking these mental steps. He must first secure the patron's favorable attention, and then arouse his interest in the goods. He must quicken the interest into a desire to buy, and finally induce this desire to action. Attention is gained through the ordinary avenues of approach to the mind, the five senses. Interest is obtained by an appeal to the feelings, and desire and action are aroused by an appeal to the will.

The method of approach to the patron's attention varies with the goods for sale. The minister, in selling his text to the congregation for its every day use, secures its attention in a widely different way from that which the newsboy with an ''Extra'' employs in gaining the attention of his patrons. Were they to reverse their methods it would be fatal to the sales in both cases. To secure interest we might find the key in the word ''personal,'' because naturally every man is interested in himself, and anything that appeals to self-interest usually gets a response. Interest belongs to the feelings, as said before, and is an internal sensation which leads toward desire, and desire is of the will, which is the ego of the man and inspires to action.

A notable example of salesmanship, illustrative of all its elements and factors involved, is presented by that master salesman, William Shakespeare. Consider for a moment the great speech which Mark Antony made to the Romans over Caesar's body: ''I come to bury Caesar, not to praise him.'' Strange! the populace expected Antony to do the ordinary thing, cry for vengeance or weep over his slain friend. This singular opening remark gained their attention. Prejudiced as he knew the rabble to be, he did not immediately defy nor antagonize them. Rather, he tactfully consented to their attitude, as made by Brutus (an honorable man), and sustained their interest by persuasive suggestions. He appealed to their patriotism by citing the occasions on which Caesar led many captives into Rome and did the general coffers fill. He resorted to specific examples of Caesar's virtues to refute the accusation of Brutus that Caesar was ambitious. Next, he excited their cupidity by mentioning Caesar's will whereby property was left to "the commons." With interest now at white heat, he inspired action by convincing arguments and persuasive words which touched their feelings and stirred them to mutiny. He successfully sold them on the proposition of Caesar's revenge, and the minds of "the commons" were brought into agreement with his at the point where they exclaimed:

> We'll burn his body in the holy place,
> And with the brands fire the traitor's houses!

When Antony saw he had made the sale, he expressed his content and satisfaction in

> Now let it work! Mischief, thou art afoot,
> Take thou what course thou wilt!

Thus we see that service can be applied only by and through salesmanship, and that salesmanship is the measure of the capacity to superinduce in the mind of the patron the four mental states of attention, interest, desire and action, before he is able to serve him.

CHAPTER IV.

THE BUSINESS MAN'S EDUCATION

Study to show thyself approved unto God, a workman that needeth not be ashamed.   —*II Tim. ii; 15.*

IT IS a great change of the mental state from the old motto of the business world, "Let the buyer beware," to the modern maxim, "He profits most who serves best." However, compared with the long period of man's residence upon the earth during which he was in a state of intellectual darkness, the step was taken in an almost infinitesimally short time, after his mind became conscious of its own possibilities and his latent energies were drawn out.

Indeed, in the drawing out, educting or educating of man's faculties lies the cause of his rapid intellectual advance. It was the appreciation of the far-reaching effects of education that inspired President Wilson to say, "Education is a thing of infinite usury; money invested in it yields a singular increase to which there is no calculable end, an increase in perpetuity, increase of knowledge, and therefore of intelligence, touching generation after generation with new impulses, adding to the sum total of the world's fitness for affairs—an invisible but intensely real spiritual usury beyond reckoning, because compounded in an unknown ratio from age to age."

Education is the development of the power to serve, and whatsoever contributes to the individual's power to serve is a part of his education. One must add something to the world's prosperity in order to merit its special esteem. Society tolerates a man who simply pulls his own weight, but it despises the man who gets from it more than he gives. It demands that every man develop his virtues and become positively industrious, positively efficient, and positively moral. It makes this demand in the face of the fact that "man is born artless in all industries, lawless in all institutions, speechless in all languages, opinionless in all philosophies, and thoughtless in all reasons."

It is not so much the capacity as it is the necessity for education that differentiates man from the animals. Human society vies with nature in demanding that man live up to his creative necessity of educating himself. "Education means the acquiring of experiences that will serve to modify inherited adjustments. Capability of education is the ability to profit by those experiences, and therefore only those experiences are valuable which render one more efficient for future action."

In the kingdom of education all roads lead to service. A great seer once said, "God is the complex of all uses, in essence love, in form a man;" and He who was greatest among men stated that He attained to that greatness wholly on the ground that He was servant of all. If this is true, man, who is made in the image and likeness of his Creator, partakes of this image and likeness insofar as he performs uses. All forms of uses are forms of service, and therefore, the kingdom of business is a kingdom of service, wherein each individual takes his position according to the degree in which he is able to serve.

There are three essential conditions to the performance of the best service. First, there must be a desire to serve; second, a knowledge of how to serve; and third, the capacity to render the service. Education, then, has to do with the development, drawing out and application of these three powers in man. Desire, inasmuch as it is of the love or will, belongs to the heart; knowledge or understanding belongs to the head; and capacity is of the body or hand. Hence, true education applies itself definitely to these three human powers.

The word *educate* is derived from the two Latin words, *e,* meaning out, and *ducere,* meaning to draw. The athlete educts or educates his muscles by drawing out their inherent power. He does this by a twofold process. First, he gives his muscles proper nourishment; second, proper exercise, and the muscles are educated to the degree in which their power is drawn out. Man's mental education is analogous to the drawing out of his physical muscles. His mental muscles are divided into three groups, so entirely distinct as to be discrete. In the first group are the muscles of his heart, which give him the desire to serve; in the second group are the muscles of his head, which give him the knowledge of how to serve; and in the third group are the muscles of his body which give him the capacity to serve.

These groups differ as degrees of altitude rather than as degrees of latitude; they are related as first, second and third; higher, mediate and lower; inmost, middle and outmost. They are like end, cause and effect, and may be thought of as a column (Figure 1), or as three concentric circles (Figure 2), or the first may be thought of as a line, the second as a plane, and the third as a cube (Figure 3). These qualities are the three essentials to anything, whether it be mental or material, and combined they make the complete unit.

The task of every business man is to develop and realize his three mental dimensions, the desire to serve, the knowledge of how to serve, and the capacity to serve. His business education, therefore, requires that mental food and exercise which will educt or draw out these three compages of his intellectual muscles. True education will give priority to the muscles of the heart, training them to desire, love, and feel those things which make for the very *esse,* or being, the ego or *I am,* or the character of the man, as the highest in the column of manhood, the inmost circle of life, the line in the cube of personality.

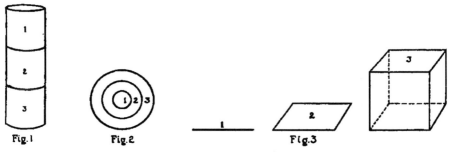

Fig.1   Fig.2   Fig.3

True education will give secondary training to the muscles of the head by nourishing and exercising them in the things that make for wisdom or ability, which is the sum of the powers to think, remember and imagine, thus forging the mediate band in the column of manhood, the middle circle of life, the breadth of personality.

True education will apply itself lastly to the nourishment and exercise of the muscles of the body, giving them the capacity to do the things desired by the heart and thought by the head, and thus form the base in the column of manhood, the outermost circle of life and the depth of personality.

As yet our educational institutions hold themselves aloof from the business world as they did in the beginning. The origin of the word *school* is from the Greek word, σχολη, meaning leisure. The leisure class of the old world, born of the nobility, enjoying governmental privileges, came together in a loafers' club for the purpose of amusing themselves in speculative thought and subtle philosophies. This idle gentry had their meeting places dubbed as *scholé*. No one was admitted to the leisure club who was under the least necessity to put forth an effort to make a living. Service was despised and all forms of labor were held in contempt. Merchants were looked upon as pirates (which indeed they were), and the marketplace was to be avoided except under dire necessity, in which event menials* did the purchasing for their masters.

The leisure clubs builded better than they knew. Their speculative philosophies resulted in experiments and application, and gradually the natural sciences absorbed and embodied the soul of this mentality, and science replaced mystery, astrology became astronomy, and the secret things of alchemy shaped themselves into the truths of chemistry. Similar transformations occurred in every department of thought, and thus was laid, too, unconsciously, the foundation on which was built the dynamic science of business.

---

*The menials were often whipped and robbed if they could not be otherwise forced into buying the vendors' wares. Indeed, the word market had its origin in the fact that an actual mark was made in the sand of the open court to separate the buyers from the vendors. In Rome over the line on the side of the latter was written the warning, *"Caveat Emptor"* (let the buyer beware).

Had the members of the Greek leisure clubs any concept of the great service they were rendering unborn generations, their antipathy for useful labor would have put them on the defensive, as most persons who despise uses are, and they would have opposed rather than abetted the function and work of the educator, and would have joined that great number of men whom President Wilson had in mind when he said, "I have undertaken the work of teaching a great many years and have found that the human mind has great resources for resisting the introduction of knowledge."

A man's education is acquired in four distinct periods, the prenatal, the parental, the scholastic, and the postgraduate.

His prenatal period reaches back to the misty shores of the "Beginning." The past pours its accumulated stores into the organic structure of his mind and body, which give him an "aptitude," "predisposition" or "talent." While the past contributes to his education in this unseen and unconscious way, it doubly blesses him by using the earth as a great storehouse in which it lays up visible treasures in the form of organized governments, and the infinite forms of uses wrought by the hands of the countless dead and held in trust for him by all the living, securely locked in the treasury of applied science, the key to which is handed to him upon his advent into the world.

The parental period of his education is that in which he is under his parents' care and is the acknowledged lord and master in the house. All about him await his wishes and more than fairy hands extend toward him with every gift he is capable of receiving, and willing feet stand ready to run to any service he is capable of enjoying. As fast as he can receive and appropriate these gifts, the willing servants pass from props without to factors within, and led by precept and example, he enters upon the third period in his education, the scholastic.

In the scholastic period he enjoys the privilege of a larger parental form in the educational institution wherein the state is his parent. He is given that mental and physical training which should prepare him for his life's activities, and when he leaves his Alma Mater, the boundless shore of the business world awaits him with the question, "Do you desire to serve?"

The fourth or postgraduate is the dynamic period in a man's education. In it he gives direction, point and action to what has been gathered in preceding periods. His success depends more upon the proper application of his mental and physical powers, and the wise investment of his mental and physical stores, than the development of these powers and the gathering of these stores. Study is not the end, but the means or preparation for his entry into the great whirlpool of human activity, in the midst of which his soul is tried and his personality is developed. He might delve into the sciences in their quiet abodes, dissociated largely from his fellows, and isolated from society without ever partaking of the sweets of human communion and fellowship, which are life's best sauce.

It has been well said that nature makes an occupation a necessity, society makes it a duty, but every man should make it his joy. The business world is the last, best and highest field for drawing out the divinely implanted capacity in man to conjoin himself with the entire race by the free and righteous exchange of the product of his own brain and hand. The dynamic force thus let loose from its static power, constitutes that magnetic personality developed in business intercourse, and the man is truly educated in the degree that he possesses the power to serve.

CHAPTER V.

THE BUSINESS MAN AS A STUDENT AND AS A TEACHER

"The most beneficent and, indeed, I might say, the most sacred labor in which man can engage is the search for Truth in the understanding of the laws that govern life; and the best that man can do for his fellows is to teach them to live in conformity with these laws."
—Anon.

AN ANIMAL is born into the knowledge of the science of its life. It need not and it cannot study. Its mind is like a garden capable of growing only a certain kind of seed, and it cannot be improved by planting any other. Its perfection is its imperfection. For instance, a bee is born into the knowledge of making honey, and it cannot be taught to spin silk. The making of honey is its sole accomplishment—its specialty—and it achieves a wonderful perfection in its function.

Man, however, is born into the ignorance of the science of his life, but with the capacity to learn and apply any or all knowledge pertaining to his welfare. His mind is like a fertile garden, in which any kind of seed may be planted and made to grow by proper culture. Man's imperfection is his perfection. His mind is his inheritance; if he will invest his talent it will render immeasurable and manifold results. He must, therefore, become a student if he wishes to realize on his inherited capability. If he would show himself a man he must become a student, for there is little difference between the man who *will not* study and the animal that cannot study.

Because of the common idea that only those who attend school and are provided with supervisors or instructors are students, we may imagine it impossible for all to become students. However, we should not be thus deterred, for there have been a great many men who never had the advantage of academic training but were excellent students. There have also been a great many men graduated from colleges who were never students. President Garfield said that his idea of a school was a log with a boy on one end who wanted to learn something and a man on the other end who was willing to teach that something. Neither the log nor the teacher is necessary for the boy to become a student.

Bacon tells us that "reading maketh a full man," but a man may be profoundly and widely read in literature and a master of many books, but if he cannot practice that which they contain, then he is like a thermos bottle and his learning of little use. A case is on record of a man whose wife taught him to read and he afterward studied law in his carpenter shop and became a successful lawyer and a good legislator. "Information gained from books," said Herbert Spencer, "is second-hand knowledge." That is, one may simply memorize what is written in a book without understanding and studying. Franklin, Burbank, Edison and many others gained knowledge at first hand which they have passed on to us in books.

The business man must not only read books, and many of them, but he must *study* to understand what he reads and see that it accords with its prototype, the book of nature. Nature has no secrets she will not readily tell her students; she tells but few to others. Every man is capable of learning if he will study. Note the marvelous case of Helen Keller, who should be classed as the eighth wonder of the world, greater than the other seven. She was born deaf and dumb and blind, and seemed thus to have been shut out forever from the field of knowledge. By faithful study and continual application she has acquired accomplishments surpassing those of many elegant society dames. She has learned to read and write and she even gives lectures and sings.

It is not the man who simply does what he is directed to do that renders the greatest service. It is not enough that he be attentive to his duties during the business hours of the day; he must give an account of that greater portion of his time spent in the absence of his supervisor and away from his business which, if devoted to study, will make him a master. A man's mind is double, somewhat like a cow's stomach. He gathers food for thought while at work or play, traveling abroad or at home, but he best studies when he quietly ruminates over the information gathered.

The function of the business man does not end with his study of those sciences and arts concerned in his daily conduct. He must also pass on his knowledge of them to his fellows in order that he may know them better. In short, the business man must be a teacher.

In the kingdom of the wise knowledge is the coin of the realm that should be dispensed widely and with lavish hand; extravagance is economy and hoarding a crime, for "that which a man hoardeth perisheth, but that which he spendeth is increased within him.'' To be a teacher means something more than to be a pedagogue. Some of the greatest teachers whose instruction has reached around the globe were not known to themselves or by others as such.

Newton taught the world the law of gravitation and its lesson will never be lost. Columbus, in a single demonstration, taught the sphericity of the globe. Fulton, Watt, McCormick and Howe are to be classed as teachers. Bell and Watson taught people to talk at a long distance; Edison taught new sounds and visions. Harriman and Hill have given lessons in great achievement for the advancement of the world's transportation systems. Rockefeller and Morgan have taught with a genius hitherto unknown, the constructive laws of economy in business organization and administration, and thousands of other brainy and clever teachers in the world of industry have given guidance to the development of natural resources and the organization of gigantic enterprises and are carrying the light of commerce into every quarter of the globe. Business is carrying its lighted torch into all the dark recesses of barter and trade. Every form of human service has been illuminated by knowledge communicated by men who have been students filled with the instinct of true missionaries. Zealous and capable instructors are carrying light into the bowels of the earth, revealing its dark corners and giving to mankind the rich treasures stored therein since the day of creation. Noisy factories, hot smelters, clanking shops, thronged marts of trade and busy counters of exchange bear evidence of great industrial teachers.

Every human being is a teacher for everyone possesses some knowledge, born of experience, that he can communicate to the enlightenment of even a king. As the poet says:

"You are better than I;
You are wiser 'tis true;
But some small thing is mine
That is lacking in you."

While everyone engaged in useful service may have some knowledge of nature's laws discovered at first hand by experience, yet there are degrees of knowledge ever widening and ascending like a spiral. He who presides over an association of workers should remember that his function of teaching increases directly with the number under his supervision. "The fierce light that beats about the throne" is lost unless the king mediates it down to and through his entire citizenship.

The relation of employer to employee is no longer that of master to slave, but is rather that of teacher to pupil. Hence it is with pride and hope that we witness now and then employers who take a deep and heartfelt interest in their employees. Many institutions are establishing schools for formal instruction where their employees are brought together at stated times and are taught how best to serve and to agree. The results have been more than were expected (as is always the case where good is the end), for many have found that the teacher was as greatly benefited as the taught, as an ancient philosopher once said, "I have learned much from all my teachers but more from my pupils."

Plagiarism as a crime is losing its terror and will continue to diminish to the zero point when men learn that no one possesses connate knowledge, but that everyone learns from those who have gone before him or are associated with him. It may be said that he who appropriates another's ideas is a plagiarist, but it should be said with greater force, that who does not is a fool and will ever remain one.

Ignorance and poverty never accomplished anything; wealth and wisdom are the handmaids of progress, and he who endeavors to help his brother to attain the latter will also help him to attain the former in the only natural and true way. The scientific business man has discovered that his greatest profit, real pleasure and true prosperity is based chiefly upon his wise guidance and the instruction he gives to others. He, then, who is most industrious in obeying this law will reap most certainly the benefits flowing therefrom, for "It is more blessed to give than to receive."

CHAPTER VI.

BUSINESS AND PROPERTY

Show me a penny. Whose image and superscription has it?
—*Luke xx:24.*

THE modern business axiom, "He profits most who serves best," leads us to inquire into the nature or form of the "profits," and the answer immediately presents itself, property, for business is based upon the ownership of property.

The desire for property is the peculiar badge of mankind, because man alone possesses it. No mineral, vegetable or animal possesses any property other than that of its own organic structure. Water possesses hydrogen and oxygen, but these elements combined in the proper proportion, *are* water; the lilies of the valley neither toil nor spin, nor do they acquire any property except that which is incorporated into their organization and becomes identical with them. The cow lies in the pasture with a full stomach, chewing her cud, content with her lot and envious of no other creature's.

Man is ever desirous of expanding his domain, and is ever seeking to better his condition through the acquisition of property. It is due to the fact that man has the desire for property that gives evidence of personality and his capacity to rise above environment. Minerals, vegetables and animals lack personality and the desire to express it, and consequently they are victims of their environment. The twentieth century man's difference from the cave dweller is measured by the property with which he has surrounded himself, and he has organized government largely for the protection and preservation of his property.

Man is possessed of a cupidity that urges him from within and gives him no rest; it matters not what he possesses, he still longs for more. His cupidity is born with him, for the first conscious act of the child is a reaching forth for things outside himself, and his first emphatic word is "Mine!" The desire for property grows with his growth and expands with his mind until the last act of the dying man is to reverently dispose of his property.

Cupidity is the banner under which the race marches to conquest and triumphs over its environment. Property is the symbol of man's infinite personality; it is prophetic of his final victory over every vice that separates him from his fellows and the development of his every virtue which will unite him in one grand solidarity of fellowship and communion with all his kind. It is the decoy which will lead him surreptitiously out of his entanglement in the wilderness of his brute nature, purged of its dross and tares, into the garden of his human nature.

It is the function of business to discipline and educate men into the kingdom of service, to lure them by reward to enter into the army of those who serve. The first reward for service that was given the servant was a negative one, freedom from the lash or whip. The horse serves, but he is driven by the whip and held in by the bit; lay down the whip and he stops; take off the bridle and he is gone. For a long time man served for similar reasons. However, as the race progressed, man's reward grew from a negative one, freedom from the whip, to a positive one, property, prompted by his innate cupidity.

When we think of property we invariably have in mind its commercial equivalent, money. Money is one of the most powerful elements in the business world. The Encyclopedia Brittannica refuses to define it, stating that every definition partakes of the prejudice of those who attempt it. It merely calls attention to its uses as that of "a medium of exchange," "a measure or standard of value."

Money has taken the place of the slave driver's whip; it has displaced the tyrant's lash and the king's sceptre. It is money that lures men into performing uses that enrich society, embellish civilization and glorify the state. It is the life blood of business, its circulating medium, the common denominator of all values, the reward of service, and a short method of bookkeeping to show at nightfall how much the community is indebted to its servant.

Despite its useful functions, money has its abuses. It is a commingling of a natural substance with human power, and as such, participates in that power's errors. He who will look at a penny will see that it is a material thing onto which is stamped the inscription of organized authority, and bears the imprinted emblems of the state. Money fails to distinguish between the natural and legal rights of men. Stoughton Cooley said, "It is a blessed thing for those who deny the natural rights of man that there are sufficient number who believe in them to preserve the natural rights for those who disbelieve in them."

To erase the superscription and blot out the image on the coin would be the destruction of government. As long as man seeks to encroach upon his neighbors' rights, and as long as one individual seeks to exploit a power or virtue that does not belong to him, or to assume an authority over another, just as long will this shadow or image remain upon the coin, and men will be forced to render unto Caesar those things which are Caesar's. Men are not yet able to give back to Caesar his image, nor to acknowledge nature's gifts to be those of God. The selfhood of man deflects God's given rights to the undeserving, and "man's inhumanity to man makes countless thousands mourn."

Money, bearing upon its face the image and superscription of proprietary rights, and being in itself one of nature's substances, has always been, is now and will continue to be the mediator between natural rights and coveted rights, the common denominator of value, the medium of exchange and evidence of deferred payments, until business will have reached its fruition and man has restored to himself his natural rights. Then, but not until then, will Caesar, the "lion," and the Romans, the "hinds," all become willing servants devoted to the common good.

It is the task of business to lead men from the chaos and darkness of conflicting interests into an order and light of mutual interests and service to one another. As an incentive to develop the desire to serve, God implanted in man the love of property. The horse knows nothing about the reward for services, for he is not a reasoning animal, but man, through his reason, sees the relation between service and reward.

As fire is the cause of the effect heat, service is the cause of the effect reward. To get heat reason directs man to gather the tinder and build the fire. A little fire generates a little heat, and more fire generates more heat. As patent as this relation is, few seem to see its perfect analogy in the relationships of reward and service. They fail to sense that a little service creates little reward, but more service more reward. Those who see the truth of this relation are busy serving and happy in the enjoyment of the resultant reward. Those who do not see it are complaining of the lack of sufficient reward, and oftimes are envious of their wiser fellows and distrustful of the Providence which presides over both.

> For life is the mirror of king and slave,
> 'Tis just what we are and do;
> Then give to the world the best that you have,
> And the best will come back to you.

CHAPTER VII.

BUSINESS, RELIGION AND GOVERNMENT

For modes of faith, let graceless zealots fight;
His can't be wrong, whose life is in the right;
In faith and hope the world will disagree,
But all mankind's concern is charity:
All must be false that thwart this one great end,
And all of God, that bless mankind or mend.

—*Pope.*

SINCE nature makes an occupation a necessity and society makes it a duty, let us investigate the relations a man's business bears to himself and to his fellows. Nature, in accordance with her immutable laws, decrees that a man follow an occupation or business in order to provide himself with the requisites of life. In his business, or in "that which occupies his time, attention and labor as his chief concern," a man finds his place, and his successful occupancy of it is his chief aim and duty.

Everything in the world occupies a place and every place is occupied by some thing. Nature knows no vacuum. The sun occupies a very high and exalted place in the center of the solar system; the earth occupies a place within that system, and within the earth each mineral, vegetable and animal has its place. The laws of occupancy are honored and glorified throughout all nature. The sea occupies its place and recognizes the bounds of the land. There is no desire among the fishes in the water for the place of the birds in the air, nor do the birds desire to dispossess the fish. Every entity has its being in obedience of the laws of order, for "the heavens declare the glory of God, and the firmament showeth his handiwork."

Only among men is there any restlessness and discontent with their positions. In the human world all are playing at the game of pussy-wants-a-corner; all are clamoring for places they are not qualified to fill; all are falling down to be trampled on by others possessed of the same ignoble ambition. Each is wholly disregardful of the others' rights; each seeks the emoluments, honor and reward that should belong to an intelligent and industrious service, without qualifying to render that service, thus dispossessing both the service and him who serves.

In the kingdom of greed there is no room, but disorder, contention and chaos. Its chambers are crowded and its walls are bulging under the pressure of the lust for gain; its doorways are jammed with the entering throng; its oxygen is consumed and stifling atmosphere suffocates and poisons. Poor houses, penitentiaries and asylums receive its victims—those who know not the way to service.

In the kingdom of service there is ample room, with order, peace and contentment. It is unbelievable that nature would give to the bee a talent to make honey, or to the silkworm the ability to spin silk, but leave man without the capacity to earn his livelihood. It is preposterous to think that the lilies of the valley are clothed and the birds of the air are fed, but man is given no power to provide for himself. Every man is born for some form of use and created for some particular service. Every man has a talent given him at birth, which, if he will discover and use, will give him a place among his fellows that will so employ and delight his every faculty he will desire no other man's place nor envy another man's reward any more than a silkworm covets the honey or the bee desires the silk. Therefore, it is man's duty to discover and perform those uses for which he was designed.

When we speak of duty we encroach upon the field of ethics wherein religion finds its subjects. Religion, literally, means "to bind again," and we find true religion in the binding together of men to God by their intelligent and faithful performance of those particular uses into which they are called. The business man, therefore, should regard the performance of the work of his calling zealously, intelligently and faithfully as his religion. His office, counter or shop is the altar at which he pours out his devotions in service to his fellow man to whom he looks for reward. The quantity and quality of his goods and the excellency of his manner of disposing of them are the sacrifices which he offers and which should be without spot or blemish as far as it lies within his power. His patrons, or the buying public, is the judge to whom he must look for approval and commendation, and his heaven is the success to be attained by faith and loyalty to the truths of his calling. His resurrection is the continual promotion he merits by faithful service.

These are the cardinal doctrines of the business man. By obeying them he earns a seat among the elect, select and sanctified of the business world, and when he lays down his life, be it long or short, he earns the right to be canonized as one of the patrons of business. Inasmuch as the science of business treats of the infinite forms of uses, it takes on a universal form that gives no offense to the worshippers of any god, desecrates no temples, but instead, directs the attention of the devotees to the service of each to the other.

If business binds a man so closely to his fellows as we have seen, it is evident that business must be subject to those laws or codes of conventional conduct which are regulated by society in the form of governments. There are five kinds of governments which are related in a causal way, since each grew out of the one before it. The first form of government descended from the deity in the form of austere commandments, and was called *theocratic*. From the theocratic there was born the *patriarchal* form, wherein divinely appointed supervisors directed and judged human conduct. Then in further descent the people were made the electors for the selection of a ruler from their number, and such a government was called *monarchical*. By broadening the function and enlarging the number of rulers and multiplying the legislators, limiting and defining their powers by constitutional barriers, the monarchical government became a *republic*. Finally, there is the fifth form of government, not yet perfected, which is known as an *industrial democracy*. In it, men will have reached the point of self-government, based upon the natural relation of man to man, with equal rights, equal power and equal voice insofar as this equality is guaged by the mental and industrial efficiency of the individual.

That government which is truly human is based upon the wisdom and virtue of its people, which are

determined by the three necessary attributes of the
human in the individual, namely, the desire to serve,
the knowledge of how to serve and the capacity to
serve. Such a government is an industrial democracy,
and in the vestige of the austere and superstitious
things of theocracy are found the primary, revealed,
infallible and just laws of nature; the blind dictates
of the patriarch become the clearly perceived and
formulated laws known as business science; the king
represents the fundamental principles upon which
business is built, and his scepter is efficiency; the republic is the grouping together, classification and
application of the general principles in the different
fields of labor.

Industrial democracy is the government of those
people in whom all these things are concentered, of
the individual who has found himself and is expending
his energies in useful service and who thus becomes a
true soldier of the common good, distinguishing himself only by the dignity and nobility of the service
he performs.

The fundamental and basic principles of the industrial democracy is service, and its slogan is, "The
tools to those who can use them." Its declaration
of independence is, "Give to the public that which the
public creates and to the individual that which the
individual creates." The first article of its constitution is, "The earth, including all natural resources,
is the common heritage of all the people, and shall
be held sacred as the gift of the Creator to those living upon it." The second article of its constitution is
"Each individual shall enjoy the full product of his

own efforts.'' All other articles are but corallaries of these two.

When the people will have reached that degree of morality, mentality and efficiency that they will ratify this constitution and endorse its articles, then they will have become sovereign citizens of an industrial democracy, and justice will have become a reality, independence an actuality and equity a realization. And much, if not all, of the public scandal of crime, poverty and insanity will be banished from the earth.

Thus we see that government should concern itself about something more than the keeping of the peace of its citizens, waging war on its enemies and collecting taxes at home and revenues abroad. Business, too, should concern itself about something greater than wages, profits and enlarged trade, and religion should look more to the character of the man than to his punctilious performance of traditional ceremonies. Government, business and religion should bend their efforts to develop each individual as a unit in the mass of humanity. Human welfare should be made the true basis for the development of each unit so as to enable him to render the greatest service possible, and for the subordination of the individual's selfish ambition to co-ordination with the efforts of his fellows for the enrichment of society. This would bestow upon the individual the greatest blessing possible, and at the same time cause him to contribute his full share toward blessing his kind. This is but another, and the true way of enlarging manhood and building character, which is, after all, the true end of business, government and religion.

CHAPTER VIII.

NATURE—THE IMAGE OF THE PERFECT MAN

The invisible things of Him from the creation of the world are clearly seen, being understood by the things that are made.
—*Romans I; 20.*

CARLYLE said that there are only two books, nature and human nature. The first is written in the language of the natural sciences; the second has not been written, or at best only in part. We have been so engrossed in our study of the book of nature, that we have neglected the other and more important book of human nature. For this reason, let us turn our attention toward the truths of this latter book, for we shall find it broad and large, interesting, pleasurable and profitable. The proper distinction between the two fields is that the knowledges of nature are the static sciences, and of human nature, the dynamic sciences. Knowledges of the static sciences may and do advance, but their subjects are stationary, fixed and always remain the same. Knowledges of human nature increase daily, but so do their subjects. In no sense is human nature fixed, either in the race or the individual, and therefore its study is rightly called dynamic. Mineral, vegetable and animal are always the same in both subject and object, and they await their time for the magic touch of the human hand to change them. Human nature undergoes constant change from birth until death of the individual or the nation. Man is like a chameleon in that he changes in thought, feeling or expression by everything that touches him. He is never the same for any continuous

53

period of time, but constantly fluctuates more or less according to his changing environment. That does not say, however, that he is not governed by laws, principles, and powers that may be discovered, organized and taught as the study of human nature; on the contrary, it accentuates the necessity for the study of human nature if we would intelligently interpret man and follow him through all his changes and account for them.

So important is Human nature that nature has no other mission than to serve as the fixed symbols by which it may be interpreted, and the manifold uses it subserves in perfecting man. The book of nature is little more than the alphabet, mathematical characters or musical notes to be learned for the one great purpose of reading human nature, solving her problems and singing her songs. It is the book of man's life to be opened and read only by the help of the natural sciences. Natural truths are but the "dust of the ground" out of which the mind is formed and made, but it awaits the breath of life to be breathed into these dry things before it becomes a living soul.

Let no man think he is educated when he has mastered even every natural science, but rather let him think that he has only learned the alphabet and is merely ready to begin its use in reading man or human nature. "When you have learned all there is to know about business," John Graham says in substance to Pierrepont in "Letters of a Self-Made Merchant to His Son," "you have learned only one-eighth of the subject, the other seven-eighths consist of knowing human nature."

When Columbus first sighted land after his long, perilous voyage, imagine his thrill of excitement and anxiety of mind as to what else he would soon behold when safely landed on its shores. He thought he had reached India, and his experienced mind had already drawn a picture of those things he expected to behold. He was so filled with his prejudgments that he failed to recognize the strange people and things he saw as being far moved from India. The people whom he beheld, having less experienced minds, were incapable of comprehending the significance of his advent. To them Columbus was a wonder: his white face seemed to glow with the light of the sun, and they associated him with their gods. His sail boats were as phantom sea crafts; his dress, guns and other trifling accoutrements confirmed their fears that he was some supernatural being.

These "children of nature" whose minds "proud science had never taught to stray so far as the solar walk or milky way," were gullible to the fullest extent. Yes, they were the *children of nature,* and like children, were subject to her every caprice. Her smile, gentleness, spontaneous production, salubrious weather and pacific breezes were indeed her caresses and blessings. Her excessive heat, cold, drought, inundation and fierce storms and still fiercer beasts and reptiles were evidences of her anger which scared, tortured and murdered them.

As nature's children grow up in the knowledge of her laws, nurtured and admonished by them, these things pass away as many have passed away now, and as man becomes an adult Human, that is, *truly* Human, he will see nature in an altogether different light. When he directs the rays of natural science upon her phenomena, he will find that the hitherto sealed book will begin to open and unfold her mystical truths, for nature, as said above, is symbolic and significant of human nature, as the shadow is to the substance. Man is just now entering a period wherein nature is seen to be a secondary thing, a mere instrument for human betterment, and he promises to enter into his true estate as lord of nature; he is now learning to command nature by mastery of her laws and this is why the twentieth century witnesses greater progress than all the two hundred forty thousand preceding centuries. Strip from nature all that man has put on her and she would be naked indeed. There would be left no evidence of business, science, schools, inventions, government or society. Reclothe her again, and behold a vision of what has come out of man and a prophecy of what is yet in him. Great, glorious and eternal as nature is, she is but the tool of human nature and when man comes into his potential knowledge, power and use, he will recognize her as such.

However, let us not dwell upon the subjugation of nature to man at too great length, for it should not be looked upon as a subjugation of an opposing force, but rather as the harmonizing with a co-operating force. The perfect man will be one who has incorporated nature into himself and henceforth sees it within him, as a mirror incorporates the image which is seen within it. Nature is the image of the perfect man and she holds herself before him as the perfect representation of what is in him.

Columbus and his newly found friends were alike in that both were the children of nature, for nature was everywhere *without* to both of them. They differed only in that Columbus had more knowledge of nature and her laws, and hence more of nature had come *into* him, making him a larger and better man. We have already begun to discern that nature's light and darkness are symbolical of the instructed and uninstructed mind, a mind luminous with truth or dark with ignorance. Nature's ups and downs are sensibly seen to prefigure man's mental exaltation or abasement; her electric and magnetic forces are symbolic of the driving and drawing power in man; her acids and alkalis are evident in the active and passive dispositions of people; and her mineral, vegetable and animal qualities are in evidence in all their varieties in all men. So universal is this truth that human nature affords a field for the application of every scientific truth, and in addition, opens a new vista of inexhaustible and superior truths to the student.

Shakespeare was a master student of human nature and his plays are mostly expositions of it. Indeed, nearly all dramas, both comedies and tragedies, are illustrative lessons of human nature. There have been many other eminent students of human nature, Dante, Milton, Swedenborg, *et cetera*, but none ever organized his knowledge and as yet an exposition of the science remains unwritten. It is possible that the Bible may be found to reveal more of its secrets than can be found elsewhere outside of its subject, man. It is said of Jesus, that "He knew what was in man." He doubtless did know, but he did not teach his knowledge openly, but by parables and it may be that when these parables are opened and explained by a true human science we shall obtain the knowledge we covet. And it may be that the whole Bible, which contains many parables, and allegories, some of which we all admit are yet sealed to our eyes, will, when opened, reveal the knowledge for which we search. He who writes the science of human nature will render a greater service to mankind than has ever yet been rendered by any writer. "The proper study of mankind is man" was not an idle remark of a jester, but the serious and solemn conclusion of one of the world's greatest poets and students.

Man and his knowledge are two distinct things: he would not be what he is without his knowledge, nor could there be a receptacle for knowledge without man. The source of knowledge is not within man, but beyond and above him. It makes him what he is by operating in and upon his responsive organs. At every lifting up of a faculty prompted by a desire to know, there is instantly a sense of touch with a creative life and consciousness is born within. Knowledge is higher than man, and its influence and effect is creative of him and instrumental in making, shaping and forming his character and life. When a man has "found himself" in the midst of a mighty universe he has made a very important find; when he knows nothing beyond what he calls his own knowing, he is then in the minimum degree of his being. To find himself in fullness, he must ally himself with laws and forces that are not his own and to which he must bow in reverence and hope that he may come out and expand himself until he becomes one with these larger things.

It is nature reflected in man that elevates, broadens and gives just and true proportions to his manhood. If we could imagine a man who was perfectly familiar with all of nature and master of her laws, we would image a perfect man. Probably there will never be such a man, nor need there be, for man does not find his strength and wisdom in himself alone, but shares it with his fellows and they share theirs with him.

One is impressed when visiting the many and well organized industrial and mercantile establishments of today, with the efficiency of the workers as a whole and the power of their aggregate knowledge. For instance, visit a shoe factory and consider the men making shoes. Think of the excellency of the product issuing from the plant and it seems nothing short of a miracle that from the sum of the wisdom of the multitude of men, each of whom seems to know but little yet knows that little well, a product could come forth the faultless and perfect child of corporate wisdom without bearing upon its features some birthmark of the individual ignorance of the great number of workers in and about the plant. Probably not a single man in the factory ever drove an ox or fed a steer. An invoice of the ignorance of the men in the plant would seem to be enough to darken and hide the face of the sun that illuminates them in their work from the reception of the raw hide to the addressing of a box of goods sent to some far-away merchant.

Inasmuch as man becomes man by progressively learning of nature, he also becomes more a man by union with his fellows, thus forming a compact more truly human in the development of a new relation or association, a kind of corporation, or one body, including many men. In this corporation in which several individuals fuse and melt into one mass, adding the mental acquirements and sharing the one with the all, and the all with the one, wisdom and strength is multiplied and a greater power and fuller life is enjoyed by all. In the natural laws, "In union there is strength," and "The injury of one is the concern of all," it is easy to see the perfect fellowship or society which on a larger scale will reflect nature; and the individualities of the many may be seen in the larger and grander man.

Creation prepares man in its own image and he may see himself mirrored and reflected in boundless nature. Before the image can be of true proportion, he must be developed in every faculty that goes to make the complete organism of man. He must possess an all around sensitiveness, and discernment of the uses of the infinite things of nature before he can become the conscious embodiment of the things in him which nature holds forth before him as in a mirror. When every organ in man is responsive to every particular thing in nature, he is like a harp whose strings vibrate at the touch of the musician, and he is the complete, the perfect man. Science, art and philosophy, must each sound their cords in order that man may come into his perfect estate.

There is an unearned increment, a residue and usury resulting from the co-operation of several which does not accrue, nor is possible, to the several working separately. It is this residue, unearned increment or usury which enriches corporations, societies, and the world. This truth is patent to every business man. It is the business man to whom we look with confidence to organize fragmentary truths of nature, found a little here and a little there, a little in this man and a little in that man, into one grand whole or great corporation and thus cash in on the accumulated truths exploited from nature, plus the accumulated experiences exploited from men in every field of work, leading to the perfection of man.

One of the world's foremost business men, a multimillionaire, who made his millions because he has obeyed the laws of nature, acknowledged his gratitude to his employees, developed the efficiency of his workers and restored the degenerate to honest producers, recently sought to restore mad Europe to sanity by persuading the warring nations to stop violating nature's laws in the interest of their own welfare. He sought to re-enlist the nations in the world's work and to hasten the coming of the day when all shall be freed from the beast in man wherein the human is planted and is struggling to come into its own.

When men are drawn together by nature's laws into a union, every advantage flows to all within it, and as "in a multiude of council there is much wisdom" so more of nature is reflected in this greater man, and he is able to rise above her caprice, harness her forces and compel her to render a greater service and a surer sustenance. Should all the people of this globe pool their knowledge of nature and her laws and work together for mutual ends, nature would be well nigh conquered and mankind delivered from her tyranny. When nature has unfolded all her secrets and taken man into her confidence, they will be one, for nature is the image of the perfect man, who reflects her perfection. Nature is human law in the natural world and man is natural law in the human world.

CHAPTER IX.

THE IDEAL WORLD IS ONE OF SCIENTIFIC BUSINESS RELATIONS

America asks nothing for herself but what she has a right to ask for humanity itself. —*Woodrow Wilson.*

THIS is a mixed world of many men with many minds. Under present conditions it is too much to expect universal peace, harmony and happiness to reign. We have been too long following expediency rather than truth. Dr. Frank Crane said, "Every animal has its parasite, every living organism has its peculiar destructive microbe. The name of that particular bacillus which eats the life out of truth is *expediency*. The minute one asks, 'What's the use?' he ceases to be a scientist, an artist or a moral person. For ages the world's highest thinking, or rather its thinking upon highest themes, was conducted along immoral lines. For men have asked not, 'Is it so?' but 'Is it advisable to say that it is so?' It is modern science that has laid the world under an everlasting debt, by standing out for the theory that what is true must always and absolutely be best for us to know and to follow. Few realize that intellectual honesty is a modern discovery. Any system built on non-facts becomes a breeding ground for tyrannies and morbidities." In the interest of the science of business, let us ignore expediency and proceed by making a proper analysis and see what facts, forces and conditions we have to deal with, then we can estimate them approximately and outline a "budget," which will make proper allowance for the action of each factor. In this way we will come nearer attaining the goal than if we go it blindly, depending upon fate to take care of mistakes. Progress is possible only by the faithful following of the ideal.

Men are beginning to be interested in this problem for the first time in the world's history, because they are forced to its consideration by the growth of business which is becoming universal in extent. Business has so overgrown mere individual, local, state or even national rights that these are made secondary to what may be termed world rights, or human rights.

The world needs a new Magna Charta or Bill of Rights that will give assurance of success to any man or organization of men that proposes to carry out a scientific program based on natural law, without being in danger of being pronounced an outlaw. He should be encouraged to do good by following nature's laws regardless of organized efforts of ignorance to hinder. Nor does this mean empirical dominion, but tried, true, philosophical and scientific dominion recognizing the right of natural law to run and be glorified on all planes wherever it may appear. Such a dominion would make a near, if not an exact approach to a theocracy (not as in the beginning when God was supposed to govern the world in person by his arbitrary authority), wherein God governs through the agency of man qualifying in knowledge of nature's laws—a kind of *vox populi est vox Dei* in an industrial democracy. The common good is put above every form of private good and the earth taken as the boundary of the kingdom, scientific business is the form of government and individual efficiency the official badge.

The end our ideal leads us to is the good of all and must be kept constantly in mind. In consideration of the problem from whatever angle, the common good must be put above every form of private good. Our ideal reaches beyond the narrow limits of family, tribe or nation and extends until it includes no less a field than the planet. We must enlarge our faith and extend our charity with confidence until we know not only that two and two are four, but that nature's laws are inviolable. There are two factors underlying the largest success of men co-ordinating their efforts on any and all planes for any purpose. The first is universal and social and is *the spirit of co-operation*. The second is particular and individual and is *the efficiency of those who co-operate*. The former broods over the latter to give it birth; men may come and men may go, but society goes on forever. The latter glorifies the former in the degree in which it does honor to the spirit from which it is born. The development of the efficiency of the individual is a factor that must be attended to, for the perfection of the whole stands upon the perfection of each part. Let us now address our attention to the tools we must use in our attainment of the ideal.

The raw materials which nature has abundantly given us in the form of natural resources, should be free at all times for the use of the present inhabitants of the planet and not kept as an heirloom or withheld from use. The only title to them is occupancy or use, an inalienable title that nature has decreed cannot be passed to another under any condition without disturbing the natural rights of man and dividing society into two parts, the House of Have and the House of Want, thus poisoning the waters at the fountain head and creating universal sickness. The only deed one needs to sunlight is a pair of good eyes; if he has these, all the sun is his. A hint to the wise is sufficient. By the same reason, he should be left in freedom to make use of any and all natural resources with which man is supplied.

Natural resources are multiplied and made available by mechanical laws. For instance, eye-glasses, the product of the thought and labor of man, when assisting nature, magnify her powers. The man who made the glasses is entitled to wear them in preference to any and all other men. Now, if one man finds he can produce eyeglasses more easily and with greater delight than he can grow a bushel of potatoes, and another man finds his pleasure and use producing potatoes, they can exchange their product on their own terms without injury to either and to the betterment of both. In a general sense and on a grander scale, the knowledge and application of mechanical laws is a tool to be used in working for the ideal.

When mechanical laws operate and enlarge upon natural resources and men exchange their products, the problem of a proper unit of value presents itself. No individual has the right to make any standard of value, weight or volume. That is a purely social or governmental function. A scientific judgment would take no notice of the value of the standard itself. A standard simply makes for accuracy, convenience and justice, and as man's relations become more universal, his standards must be recognized by all nations and languages alike. Science knows no such limitations as bind the commercial world. Scientists speak and think in a universal tongue, understood by all, and if the commercial world wishes to progress, it must follow a similar course and become a world of scientific business relations. The unit, let it be whatever it may, will be called simply one measure, one weight, or one value.

When man has effectively used the tools of natural resources, mechanical laws and universal standard of exchange, he will have attained the ideal. The complex problems of individuals, corporations and governments will have been solved, and much, if not all misunderstandings, contentions and disputes will have passed away; the chief cause of theft and crime will have been removed and the dark and dismal clouds of subtle advantage, covetousness and legal wrongs will have passed away, and the bright light of open and fair dealing will shine with a greater force; and honesty and good intentions will beam from the face of all men. Education will mean qualification for efficient service and religion will mean living well. The philosophy of business concerns itself only about those matters which make for universal peace, happiness and content. Its contention is for nothing less than the rights of humanity and no individual, corporation or nation can come into greater honor than by rendering obedience to those laws inspired by this ideal.

CHAPTER X.

THINKING

Thy wish was father to that thought.

—*Shakespeare.*

BUSINESS is constructive, progressive, and productive, and to pursue it successfully one must have initiative and originality. The source of all action is in thought, and therefore the business man must be a thinker. Let us examine the process of thinking, and seek to understand, if possible, its operation, so that we may know where we are.

The copy books we used in the penmanship class in school had us write the legend, ''The wish is the father of the thought,'' until every letter was indelibly impressed upon our minds. It is in this old adage that we find the key to thought—in the wish, or more explicitly in love. Love is the father of thought, nature is the mother, and all knowledges are the children of the union.

The word *philosopher* literally means a ''lover of wisdom.'' Burbank, a natural philosopher, loved flowers and by close communion with them and study of them, he has understood the ''language of the flowers'' and they have told him many secrets, which they have told no other man. He has loved them, believed in them; he has been patient, gentle, kind and tender with them, and has proved that he is their friend and companion. They have responded by opening their dumb mouths and telling him of their desires, ambitions, capabilities, loves, passions, and potency, how they longed for nuptial relations to propagate their kind and improve their species. They revealed to him the commandments and laws written in their organic structure to increase and multiply and fill the earth with beauty, fragrance and loveliness. The flowers told all this to Mr. Burbank, their lover, and they made a thinker of him.

The same thing has taken place with every other thinker who has given to the world anything worth while. And it is what every man must do if he, too, would contribute to the world wealth that can never be destroyed, and in so doing he will live forever in the affection of his fellows. Columbus wooed from the earth, by a life of passionate devotion, the secret of her shape; Newton wooed the most subtle secrets from the boundless universe and she, in answer to his ardent love, unfolded all nature's laws. Franklin was enamored with a thunder cloud and she stooped and kissed his lips. Thus we see the love of wisdom as the father, nature as the mother and knowledge as the child.

When one comes into the world his mind is a blank without form or content. Surrounded by all the things the material world puts at his disposal, he is unaware of their existence; he does not recognize their forms nor their uses. He is passive, receptive, and awaits to react to their actions. They are the teacher and he is the learner. They must open their dumb mouths and speak, introduce themselves, be conveyed into his mind. Their purpose is to instruct, inform and construct his mind. Things teach man; man does not teach things. The shining sun taught man to see: vibrating things taught him to hear; odoriferous things taught him to smell; things with resistance taught him to feel and savory things taught him to taste.

How do things teach man? How do they introduce themselves into his mind, leaving their images until his whole mind is a mental photograph of the whole world, there to remain and grow forever? Surely no material thing can enter through the mystic doorways of the mind, for there is not room if man's mind is within him to contain the things of time and space. Instead, they undergo a reconstruction, a transmutation and are drawn into the mind by the powerful suction it puts forth in its thirsting for knowledge, which is insatiable, and which demands more the more it is fed.

The mind is far removed from the material world, bearing a relation as ''in'' to ''out.'' Thought is within man, things are without. The distance between the mind within and the body without is bridged over by a subtle fluid which partakes of a mental substance and a material form, and which is called the *animal spirit* for lack of a better name. This animal spirit is clothed with a very fine and pure substance called the brain, a more familiar and acceptable term. The brain extends itself to every part of the body and terminates in little mouths called nerve ends. There are an infinite number of nerve ends, but most of them are gathered and congregated into four large mouths, or centers, while the rest are distributed over the body and come to the surface in openings too small to be seen by the unaided eye. The four large openings are known as the mouth (taste), ear, eye and nose.

The scattered openings collectively give us the sense of touch.

Everything that gets into the mind must come into it through these doorways. Material things, of course, are too crass to enter the mind, but as said before, they undergo a transmutation, owing to the strong suction that the mind puts forth to draw them into itself. They leave their bodies behind them and enter only as to their souls, so to speak, and then they assume new bodies and arise to a newness of life and become immortal, and live forever as spirits in the mind. In short, they undergo a sort of death and resurrection. Let us examine this extraordinary process by taking a specific example.

Here is a piece of crayon. You see it, and when it drops onto the table you hear it. You feel it with your fingers as smooth, and round, and it crumbles with little pressure. It has an alkaline taste in the mouth and it smells dusty. If the crayon is hidden, you can still see it, hear it, feel, taste and smell it. Why? Because its photograph or image is in your mind, a mental replica of the material crayon, but not actually the crayon itself, although possibly, nearly as distinct. This mental crayon is your property and cannot be taken from you. You made it through the agency of your five senses which bridged the gulf between the material crayon and your brain. If the attention be fixed upon a single object for a given time, a clear impression of the object will be made on the mind. An after effort to *think* of that object will result in a reproduction of its qualities, such as, size, color, weight, substance, etc. Through the five senses not only this crayon, but everything may pass from out of the world of matter into the world of mind, producing what we may call *images.* Thinking, is the process of division 'and relation of parts, qualities and functions. Discrimination is peculiarly the function of thinking, and thinking is based upon sensations.

Here is another crayon, differing in size, color and form from the first. It forms into another image, a third does the same thing, and so on until you have several images of like things differing only in details. With these images in mind, you are able to distinguish a crayon from other objects and to classify it as such. Your group of images is in itself a unit, defining pretty definitely your conception of a crayon, and for this reason, we shall call the group of images a *concept.*

A concept is the unit of thought, for concepts are the things from which thought is made. We have just seen how the concept crayon was formed in the mind. All concepts are formed in the same manner. Now when several concepts are combined as were the images, we have an *idea.* An idea is a thought on the lowest or outermost plane, a thought of the first degree. It is usually composed of three or more concepts, as for instance, ''Crayon is white.'' The three concepts, *crayon, is* and *white* enter into this idea. If we pursue this subject further we find that there are three kinds of concepts, concrete, verbal and abstract. The idea above contains a representative of each kind.

All things, both natural and mental, are concrete concepts, as *crayon, rock, wood, plant, animal,* etc. A verbal concept is one concerning the *state of, action,* or *being,* and is expressed by words such as *walking, do, is,* etc. An abstract concept qualifies and modifies and is expressed by words such as *white, sour, rough, loud, pungent,* etc. The last named are called abstract concepts, because, aside from the things they qualify, they have no existence. There are no such things as white, sour, rough, etc., but *things* may be white, sour, and rough.

When two or more ideas are presented and two or more of the concepts in them differ, or agree, we contrast or compare them and discern the difference or agreement, and from our observations draw a conclusion called a *judgment,* a thought of the second degree. Let us take the two ideas "Crayon is white" and "Crayon is black." Suppose we ask the question, which is better? The answer calls for a new mental process, the formation of a judgment. If it is for the purpose of writing on a blackboard, we say that the white crayon is the better. That is a judgment, like which we form many in the course of a day, and the quality of the judgments we make measures our success. Nothing is so valuable to the man of business as good judgment, the ability to form thoughts of the second degree.

Why is white crayon better for writing on a blackboard? To answer this question we must go further than a judgment, and find a *law:* "The greater the contrast, the greater the distinction." If the business man forms sound judgments he should be able to deduce the laws on which they are founded. A law is a thought of the third degree.

When we have discovered that similar actions or events always produce the same result, we recognize a law as governing the situation. If we go further and seek the why or reason for the law, we find a *principle* underlying, and that principle is use. Use is the principle behind creation. The whole natural world is nothing but infinite forms of uses. The whole business world is nothing but an infinite form of use or service, and buying and selling are nothing more than the exchange of service in one form for another. There is no such thing as a useless thing in nature; some things we can define only in terms of the uses they perform, as for instance, electricity. This principle of use is the pinnacle of thought, and in considering it many able minds have stumbled and great has been their fall. It is the Shekinah of the mind, the inmost of being. Angels can do no more than think in terms of the principle of use, and God Himself can be no more than that principle. In the language of another, "God is the complex of all uses, in essence love, in form a man."

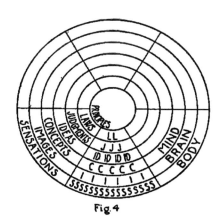

Fig. 4

Figure 4 is a diagram of the degrees of thought showing how from many sensations the mind forms images, which it combines into concepts, and by combining two or more concepts it gets an idea, several of which warrant the conclusion of judgments, from which laws can be deduced, and behind the laws are found the underlying principles.

CHAPTER XI.

MEMORY AND IMAGINATION

From nature's chain whatever link you strike,
Tenth or ten thousandth breaks the chain alike.

—Pope.

THINKING involves something more than the receiving of sensations and converting them by degrees into images, concepts, ideas, judgments, laws and principles. It also involves the recording of these stages of thought in what we know as the *memory,* so that they may be used over and over again as occasions arise. They form a subsoil, base or foothold for future mental activity, and from them arise the "children of the brain," in what is known as the *imagination.* The memory is a history of the past; the imagination is a prediction of the future. Together, they enable man to rise above his environment, for without them, he would be as obedient to fate as the animals, and submissive to the dictates of nature instead of her master.

The memory is the storeroom of the mind where a record of all sensations, images, concepts, judgments, laws and principles is kept in safe and secure reserve for instant use. If one could only think in the sense of gathering thought material and transforming it into thought, he would have no past nor future. Present thought would be of no use for future thinking, for the temple of thought might grow mountain high in a day, like Jonah's gourd, only to be cut down at night by the worm of forgetfulness. The memory is like a filing cabinet which will receive and record anything that is put into it; and the things recorded are subject to recall by

the mind which recognizes them as the record of the
things originally thought. Thus man has a past as well
as a present, and it can be brought into the living present and made a part of it. Experiment and experience
are thereby rendered valuable and wisdom increases
with age.

If one will train the memory to increase its capacity,
his power of thinking will also increase and he will be
able to serve better. The memory should be educated,
given proper nourishment and exercise. It should not
be treated as a waste basket nor overburdened with un-
necessary tasks. It should be trained according to certain laws which will lead it in the way that it should
go. The first is the law of *attention*. If one wishes to
remember a particular thing he should give the closest
attention to it so that the memory can form an accu-
rate and well defined impression. If it is a thing of or
pertaining to a substance, an apple say, the five senses
should do their part in making a clear mental image.
If it is a thing of or pertaining to a state of being or
action, as an historical event, the feelings or one's mental reaction (interest) to the thing should impress it
upon the memory.

Sometimes the closest attention is hard to give, or
one's interest is negative in the thing to be remembered.
In such a case one should resort to the law of *repetition*
and *use* in order to assist the memory. We all learned
the multiplication table in this way, and possibly our
history dates and Sunday School golden texts.

The third law is the most common and for most
minds the best way for remembering, the law of *association*. Things are easily remembered when they are

associated with other things already recorded: (a) as to cause and effect, (b) as to contents, (c) as to contrast, (d) as to contiguity, (e) as to correspondence. An example of each will suffice for an explanation.

We remember vividly the shock that we once received when we picked up a very ordinary looking wire, and since then, we have avoided careless handling of loose wires. In fact, if some one mentions live wire, we even recall the room in which we had our shocking experience, remembering the room from its contents. By contrasting two wires, one insulated and the other bare, it is easy for us to distinguish the dangerous one. Every time we see a switch we remember our live wire disaster, owing to the close contiguity of a switch to that wire. We are cautious to avoid entirely, or at least to investigate all other wires before grasping them, because they are likely to be live, corresponding to the one of our first experience.

Aside from the law of association there is the law of *suggestion* which is useful to the memory. A thing "that reminds us" usually recalls for us some other thing of a similar nature. Prompters behind the scenes in an amateur theatrical furnish suggestions to the embryo thespians.

Memory, of course, has its enemies, the greatest of which are time, disuse and diversion. Too long an interval between the recording of a thing and its recall may obliterate it from the memory. Desuetude, also, robs us of many things we should like to retain. How many college graduates in business remember La Place's Theorem? Then, too, if the mind is diverted while attending to one thing it is greatly handicapped in remembering that thing. In our young days did not all of us often forget what our mothers sent us to the store for when we met an organ grinder with his monkey that diverted our attention? But let us not dwell upon the negative side of the subject of memory, but rather turn our thought toward the product of memory, the home of the "children of the brain," the *imagination*.

Imagination is future thinking. It is that which gives life to all things. The child's imagination enables it to feel the breath of life in potato pigs in a corn-cob pen, or by it the child perceives volition and action in its sawdust doll. The imagination takes no account of the body of things; it confuses the dead with the living, the body with the soul, the apparent with the real, the conscious with the unconscious. If it is not disciplined by the other faculties it leads to exaggeration, deception, fanaticism and insanity. Great and powerful as the imagination is, it is the best of servants and the worst of masters.

The imagination is the mind's designer and architect. It builds upon the things of the memory and the present, the things to be. It projects the ideal and the other faculties verify or disprove. It plans and designs; the other faculties furnish the material and execution. It is the pathfinder, the others follow. It seizes hold of the things sensed, read, recited, thought or dreamed and claims them as its own. Mr. Edison says, "Science is mostly imagination. It is by conceiving what might be before one has seen the way to realize it practically that scientists have been buoyed during the period of experiment. The imagination . . . is the missing link between what we know and what we hope to know."

If we call thinking our mental factory and memory our mental storeroom, we may call imagination our mental laboratory or assembly room. In it we design, decide, plan, project, and experiment, bring together all mental things and fit, shape, select and assemble the several parts; we try new combinations of concepts; we rebuild, alter, test and invent. The imagination, therefore is an instrument of progress.

There are two kinds of imagination, reconstructive and constructive. The reconstructive enables us to build again in the mind that which has been built outside of it by nature or some other mind. It is the power that enables one to imitate and to reproduce in words or deeds the words or deeds of other persons or things. The constructive imagination is that power of the mind which enables it to combine into new forms, hitherto not in existence, the material gathered by the mind. Although both kinds of imagination are useful, the constructive is particularly valuable to the business man, for it renders him progressive, encourages him to work for his ideals and helps him build, by new ideas, his own power.

A man equipped with a good and reliable memory and a healthy imagination is in a fair way to success, providing he uses them properly, fights off the enemies of the memory and holds his imagination in check by his other faculties, but does not stunt it.

CHAPTER XII

THE WILL

The cause is in my will.
Shakespeare.

MINERALS grow by accretion; they are wholly passive to and unconscious of the action of outside laws and forces which cement atom to atom. The whole mineral kingdom has been constructed by powers unfelt during aeons of time. Vegetables grow as unconsciously as do minerals, in obedience to environment, but they have an internal life principle which receives and organizes dead substances into their own particular form of life. Animals grow in a like manner, but they possess an additional power, choice, and they receive or reject, to a limited degree, the food that is presented to them, or they go in search for what they do not find on the spot where they come into life.

Man's growth, besides taking place in the same manner as does a mineral's, a vegetable's and an animal's, is governed by his reason, which is adjoined to his *will*, which transfers him from the passive state to one of action. The crown and glory of manhood is not in man's passive powers and virtues, but in his conscious, rational choice, born of his will and ultimating in words and deeds which reveal the human in him as master of the mineral, vegetable and animal without as well as within himself.

Man's growth is by a dual process. The first is the process of formation or making; the second of reformation or creation. The first of course, must precede the second, but this precedence is not universal, but particular: *i. e.,* the whole work of the latter is not suspended until the whole work of the former is finished and complete. But when the former has worked howsoever little, the latter begins to work with more or less vigor. Thus these two forces conspire to work together for the perfecting of man's development.

Heretofore, we have conceived of nature as the active power and man as the passive. We now wish to reverse the emphasis and call attention to man as the active and nature as the passive; not that this is absolutely true as we represent it, for we cannot present these truths simultaneously although they act together.

The human in man is due to the development of his will, that which makes him aware of an act involving choice. The feelings alone are infantile. A child is governed entirely by them as far as his own acts are concerned; but as he grows older the knowledge he gains is his pride, and he is ashamed to display his feelings. The boy boasts of his wisdom but scorns emotions or feelings as childish. When he becomes a man, it is deeds that count more than knowledge, and he measures other men more by what they have done than by what they know. The truly manly function is not merely to feel nor seek after knowledge, but from the possession of both, to perform some useful act. When this act is one of service to his fellow men from an intentional motive, we attribute to him the distinctive quality of *human,* which places him in a class to himself and elevates him above his mineral, vegetable and animal nature to that of *homo.* Environment alone, or the first process, formation, does its work to make man an *ego.* The second process, reformation, begins to reform or create him into a *cosmo*. Let us illustrate these processes by a potter and his clay. Although the vessel may be marred before it leaves his hands, the potter can remould and reshape the clay into a new or another vessel. Man's mind is the clay and his will is the potter. Nature fixes the vessel by fire into a hard and fast form, but the mind never becomes so fixed. Man can at all times remould, reform and reorganize his mind into more desirable forms. The will is the mental power that enables him to do it.

The forming or making process produces *individuality*. The reforming or creating process produces *personality*. There is a wide difference between the two. A horse has individuality, but not personality. A man has individuality and personality; he forever retains the former, but his personality may undergo a continued change.

Individuality is defined, limited and finite; personality is undefined, unlimited and infinite. The man proper as distinguished from his animal form is the product of his personality working in and through his individuality. He is a dual being, sometimes governed by his outer and sometimes by his inner self. As an individual he is *e pluribus unum* (one among many); as a personality he is *plus in uno* (many in one). That is, there is but one personality, but myriads of individualities. For instance, Mr. Ford is one among the many Americans that go to make up Uncle Sam. David Lloyd George is one among many Englishmen that go to make up John Bull. In a similar but higher degree there is only one personality—*man*. John Smith is an individual as distinct from Bill Jones, but John Smith and Bill Jones are one inasmuch as each is included in the word *man*. Each man, insofar as he is a *homo* (i. e., insofar as he lives above his mineral, vegetable and animal nature) is one with every other man. He is but a sector of a sphere having a common center with all other sectors; or he is but one of an infinite number of rays of light radiating from a common source.

As a man's body is a receptacle for heat, his mind is a receptacle for love. Man does not create heat; he only receives and directs it. Neither does he create love, for it flows into him and is received and directed by his will. Whatsoever a man loves he wills and, if left in freedom, says and does. Every man is happy in his own loves, and that is the same as having his own will, provided his love and will are human.

A man truly human puts his family, country and race above himself, and no man is truly human who does otherwise. The human in a man is measured by the degree in which he prefers others to himself. To desire the common good is to become one with others. Those who love the common good come into the will to serve, for "No man is of sound mind unless use he his occupation." The greatest is he who wills to serve all. He who has not the will to serve cannot be educated, for true education has relation to service, and men attain manhood by and through service.

CHAPTER XIII.

THE SECRET OF SUCCESS

In all vital action the manifest object and purpose of nature is that we be unconscious of it.   *—Carlyle.*

SUCCESSFUL men and women cannot tell the secret of their success. Many have attempted it but in every case their efforts have been in vain, not because they wish to deceive us, but because they are unable to tell us. That it is a secret deeply hidden from those who fail is to be expected, but it tests our credulity to say that it remains unknown to those who succeed.

Ask the first ten successful men you meet the secret of their success, and instead of acknowledging that they do not know, they will fabricate some pretty maxim they imagine responsible for it. If the first man you question was naturally lazy but made a great effort to make himself industrious, he will say, "Industry, my boy, will put you where I am." If the second man is proud of his blood and boasts of his ancestry, he will attribute his success to the sterling character and talents he inherited from his forbears. If the third is without pride of ancestry and is self-made, he will tell you that his own acumen won him laurels. Thus every successful man will attribute his success to those virtues of which he is most conscious, that cost him the greatest effort to acquire, while he will overlook many other qualities, which were, more than likely, greater factors in his success. J. P. Morgan, John D. Rockefeller, William L. Douglas, John W. Gates, G. W. Cable, Henry Clews, Rev. C. H. Parkhurst, President Benjamin Ide Wheeler and Charles W. Elliott are among those who have endeavored to tell the secret of their success for the benefit of the experts and the public. Their answers are all inane and puerile.

We cannot rely upon the introspection of successful men for reliable information concerning the secret of success for the same reason that we cannot examine our own hearts. The heart is the most vital of all bodily organs, and thoughts about it influence its action. The skilled physician endeavors to catch the patient off his guard to ''feel his pulse'' for the conscious knowledge of the patient modifies the action of his heart. The brain, too, is a vital organ whose action is only perfect in the degree that the mind is unconscious of the process of thinking while thinking. Every physician refuses to take his own medicine. It is seldom that a lawyer tries his own case; and a business man is a poor analyst of his own success. The virtues of which they are conscious so overshadow those of which they are unconscious that they are certain to be deceived. Others must analyze them, as observing students have done, and the result is more than satisfactory.

Obedience to the natural laws in the rendering of service underlies the secret of success. Every successful man has had a passion for service, and he has rendered it by consciously or unconsciously obeying its laws. Every law has a reward as well as a penalty for its observance or disobedience. One may obey a great many of nature's laws without receiving the reward of success, and he may disobey a great many others without meriting failure. In the business world the successful man is he who has obeyed and kept inviolate as many natural laws as possible and disobeyed as few as possible.

Nature's laws are homogeneous and co-operate with each other. Even two laws as diametrically opposed as centripetal and centrifugal forces unite in maintaining the equilibrium of a planet and holding it to its orbit. The close interrelation of natural laws leads us to discover one from another. Ideas cannot grow in an empty mind; a man cannot make use of knowledge he does not possess; but he builds more knowledge upon that which he already knows, although he may not be conscious of it. Some attribute this to the subsconcious mind, but for a better term, let us call it *influx*. It is very difficult for one to understand a foreign language unless he already knows its vocabulary, for new words bewilder him. However, with a given knowledge of its words, new words can be more easily understood because the old furnish a foundation on which to build the knowledge of the new.

Great ideas take hold of men; a great passion seizes them and carries them along to a success they seem unable to account for. It is generally true that the men who have won applause had hidden deeply within them a passion for service which bore them along in a current of natural laws underlying the service they rendered. It is in recognition of this fact that the old *Arena* had for its motto, "We do not take possession of our ideas, but they take possession of us and force us into the arena, where like gladiators, we contend for them."

The man who becomes a student of the natural laws of success, until they become implanted in his mind gives freedom to the law of influx to operate when he is the least conscious of the inflow; or as some say, he must first plant them in his subconscious mind and from its depths there will arise a passion and a power carrying him along as by a flood to success. The secret of success, then, is due to the presence of a passion for service which is moved and guided by natural laws. This is "the tide in the affairs of men which taken at its flood, leads on to fortune."

CHAPTER XIV.

THE KEYSTONE PHILOSOPHY

There are more things in heaven and earth, Horatio,
Than are dreamt of in your philosophy.
—*Shakespeare.*

IT IS the business of science to exploit *facts* and to state them with authority. Science states unequivocally that two and two are four. We pity the man who cannot or will not lend his assent to that statement. Philosophy, on the other hand, is dedicated to the exploitation of *truth* concerning phenomena as resolved into or explained by causes and reasons, powers and laws. Every man, even the fool, has his philosophy, his mental angle of vision or interpretation of events. If his philosophy is true, he is a seer, a prophet and a leader; if his philosophy is false, he is deflected from the true course according to the degree of falsity of his mental angle of vision.

A wolf looking over a map of the country cannot distinguish a railroad from a river, for it cannot form a concept or think. For the same reason the wolf is the victim of its environment, which it cannot change. Its mind is full of one kind of seed and no other can be planted. It has no history, nor can it make one. Its love, wisdom and use is inscribed on its form; its zone of life is fixed; its comings and goings are with the seasons, and it never changes, for it is born a wolf, lives and dies a wolf. It has its being on one plane; there are no ascending and descending currents to its life, no spiral movements, nor any "winding about still upward"; no degeneracy or regeneracy; no civil, moral, social or spiritual power hidden within it. If any changes come to it, they come from without and not within; by force, not by consent. The same thing is true with all animals, whereas with man, none of it is true, for man is an animal *plus*. It is the plus element in man that we propose to deal with, for it is this element that makes him capable of forming concepts and thinking.

Philosophy, as stated before, is the knowledge of phenomena as resolved into or explained by causes and reasons, powers and laws. There is a mental philosophy and a natural philosophy. The former can be presented or illustrated only by things in the natural world. The things in the world of mind differ from things in the world of matter only in *substance*. The subjects of mental philosophy are *things,* but are not *material* as are the subjects of natural philosophy. It is as if the former were within and the latter without; one of the mind, the other of the body.

The two books, nature and human nature, are only the outer and inner of the same thing. The subjects in the book of nature are dead, fixed and material; those of human nature are alive, changing and immortal. They may be represented by two globes, one we call the world of matter, the other the world of mind. (Figure 5.)

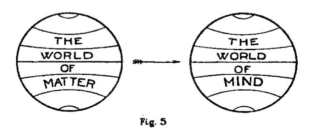

Fig. 5

The ancient philosophers called the natural world a "macrocosm," or big world and the mental world a "microcosm," or little world. They taught that there was a perfect correspondence between the two,—that all things in the natural world were signs, symbols and representatives of the things in the mental world. The ancient mythologies were based upon this doctrine, and when it was lost, their sacred books became meaningless and their teachings grotesque, absurd and ridiculous.

In the microcosm, or mental world, they called the individual unit, a man, "minimus homo," and the aggregate, or society, "maximus homo." The result of this idea we find in our modern expressions as Uncle Sam, John Bull, and other phrases which present the conception of an aggregation of individuals as a unit. Suppose we let the maximus homo, or largest man, be represented by a globe. The portions of the lines between the intersection of two parallels with two meridians bound a square, and if we imagine plumb lines dropped from the intersections to the center of the globe, a pyramid will be cut out. (Figure 6.)

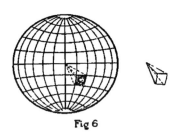

Fig 6

The sector of the globe thus formed is representative of the individual, while the globe itself represents mankind in general, society. Obviously, there are as many sectors in the globe as there are individuals composing society, and as the apex of each points to the center of the globe, so is the central aim of each individual common to all the rest, namely, *service* to the whole.

The plumb lines dropped from the intersections on the surface to the center, limit or bound the activity of the individual included between them. Therefore, in the world of humanity, each man is a keystone that supports, and at the same time is supported by every other individual. Thus we see the interdependence of men.

Suppose we carry the figure farther, and draw a cross section of the globe half way between the two meridians bounding the base of the pyramid. (Figure 7.)

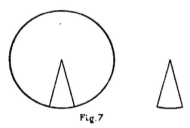

Fig. 7

Here we see the keystone as a triangle, one side of which is the arc of a circle. It represents the individual, a man, resting on the base of his five senses and surrounded by the boundless universe, and these senses gather *sensations* which unite in his brain to form images and subsequent degrees of thought.*

The geometrical simile likening society to a globe and the individual to a sector is an old idea, taught by ancient philosophers who called geometry the king

*Page 74.

92

of sciences. In fact other sciences are but the geometry of their respective things. Chemistry is the geometry of the molecules, or things in minimum; astronomy is the geometry of the planets, or things in maximum; psychology is the geometry of the mind, botany is the geometry of the seed, etc. The Greeks were the world's great philosophers. Even their alphabet has true philosophy between its first and last letters, Λ and Ω. These letters are slight departures from the forms in Fig. 7, the Alpha being comparable to the individual, or sector, and the Omega becoming the symbol of society. Thus we see the individual as the unit, the Alpha, first, beginning, initiative, etc., and society as the whole, Omega, last, and referendum, etc.

This in brief, is the Keystone Philosophy, a philosophy which includes the first and the last, the A and Z, the Alpha and Omega, the individual and the whole, the beginning and the end, the least and the greatest. There is no subject, mental or moral, political or social, spiritual or natural, that this philosophy does not encompass, and its alphabet spells the words of truth on every subject. It applies with geometrical accuracy its geometrical principles and solves its geometrical problems. Therefore, it is the keystone philosophy because it will unlock any and all doors that open into the kingdom of knowledge. The keystone philosophy anxiously awaits the demonstration of the teaching that "the kingdom of heaven is like unto a merchantman," and it looks to the business man to solve all problems, and establish a kingdom of service that will restore man to his first estate.

The keystone is that *white*[1] stone, which every man is, and in which is written that "which no man knoweth saving he that receiveth it." It is the *"foundation*[2] stone which the builders rejected" and was made the last, top or arch stone, instead of the first, *"tried"*[3] stone, or model of perfect manhood. All other stones should be like it in the building of the temple of the perfect humanity. Let society see to it that all individuals are born under just and equal conditions; that each is educated to find his proper place and then to perform the services which his occupation demands of him, thereby fitting him as a keystone in an ideal world. The result will be a society perfect in all its parts, for if the individual is made right, the family, the city, the state and the world will be right. By faithfully following the ideal, guided by the light of science as applied to business there will be developed a perfect society, which will reflect the sovereignty of God in an industrial democracy.

---

[1] Rev. II:17.
[2] Matt. XXI:42; Psa. CXVIII:22.
[3] Isa. XXVIII:16-17.

ImTheStory.com

Personalized Classic Books in many genre's

Unique gift for kids, partners, friends, colleagues

Customize:

- Character Names
- Upload your own front/back cover images (optional)
- Inscribe a personal message/dedication on the
  inside page (optional)

Customize many titles Including
- Alice in Wonderland
- Romeo and Juliet
- The Wizard of Oz
- A Christmas Carol
- Dracula
- Dr. Jekyll & Mr. Hyde
- And more...